T0312912

& Calling It Home

& Calling It Home

Lisa Cooper

chax press / 1998

Note: Poems with titles are all phonetic translations of poems by Jack
Spicer from his *Book of Magazine Verse* and *A Book of Music* (except
for one from Spicer's *After Lorca*).

Some of this work has appeared in *Blue Mesa Review, Hambone,
Logodaedalus, New American Writing, No Exit, raddle moon, 6ix,* and
Sonora Review.

ISBN 0-925904-17-1

Library of Congress Cataloging-in-Publication Data

Cooper, Lisa
   & calling it home / Lisa Cooper.
      p. cm.
   ISBN 0-925904-17-1 (alk. paper)
   1. Stein, Gertrude, 1874-1946--Poetry.   2. Women authors,
American--20th century--Poetry.   3. Authorship--Poetry.   I. Title.
PS3553.O5947A612   1998
811'.54--dc21   98-22725
                                                        CIP

to the palace of my heart—

I'm calling it home

CONTENTS

like a bride's song—
of fish, saints,
the earth, love—
wanting to sing that song forever
& calling it home

**

—red marble of love
red rage of love beating—

POOR POOR WISHES

a train headed for more mystique

Poor poor wishes
If this page is
From the same past as the giver

Why don't you pray at your age
Follower of such
Poor poor wishes

First this hand keeping gifts
Brought you white lilies
Prong marks & solid lies
Nothing is mine

Smile & stall to hide now
Dowager of such
Poor poor wishes

So while away the dog hours
Say don't stay out of kindness
Or if your matter & my matter
Appear themselves

Poor poor wishes
Tomorrow
Hell to tomorrow.

Dear Gertrude,

When the last one left, I had to invent the past.

So I'm taking him out of context. Through his words
I found the bitter man inside, saying things I
hadn't said before, but wanted to. *Jack as Jack
being Jack* heading for his own bitter implosion. As
valuable, he would say, as a rope tied to nothing.

So I pray to Our Lady, Gertrude.

What sense does it make.

One more thing, when you say *What is the use of an
unhappy anything,* when you say *Well I never had an
unhappy anything,* I feel unworthy or questioned
because a *sadness* has been my home though I
struggle to be arrested by joy & hauled out.

Love,
Lisa

INCARCERATION: A SENTENCE FOR POE

In deafening intelligence on a ruse moving
Down your conquered old self.
Would not stop for indecision. These walls
Alone are my peers, calling instead of
Old or rough fixes, old keyholes,
Old emotion. An absolute void, dreaming
Like a fresh thorn.
There is not even a north or south. Conquered
& old, disappear. My hand conjures the throat
& doesn't stop in this version. Or fix
To bother keyholes, old emotion—I'm just
Moving.

A VALLEY IN TIME

To cast a valley in time
In winter
Spend your lovers.
Spice stumbling illicit
From home
Stakes this valley in time
With wild spiked thyme.
Whether tis better
At any limit.

Dear Gertrude,

Jack's music, & choosing the birds that sing long
notes to the night after everyone's gone inside.
Those notes.

And what's on the inside & what's on the outside
for Jack. He got out of his body.

The church says not to fall for these folk figures,
there's too much credit given the saints & they
make the people superstitious. And that includes
St. Jack.

They asked if my sin was loving him more than God.
I said love is the *way* to God. Ask Mary.

Love,
Lisa

ERRATA

In any event
How we face a teen's free violence
& harken to call it diplomacy.
A hunch to tether a cub
Over to a big rock. Daring-to-die dreams.
Pain lessons. The knowing ring-bearer.
Engaged, now all the mischief is grief.

So Gertrude,

Is faith solid, liquid, or gas?

I have these fundamental questions—is it okay to
keep hoping—like believing in miracles—or is it an
insult to the present—as if you had a choice.

Do I have to wait until I am healed to start being
happy. Is there some law. Or can I be happy now in
my wounded, fallen state.

Singing a love that sings a long solo into the
night, long after everyone's gone. *That* song.

Like after surgery. Certain cuts have been made so
now you're healing. Eventually you won't even think
about it, but meanwhile your scar will ache, &
sometimes things will glue up wrong inside you so
there's that to deal with.

Who said the unconscious isn't patient enough for
poetry.

ORTHO

Carping & narrow orphan of
Joints, this movement down.
Dwelling there
At the bottom of a deep pit.
Yield
Noting it behooves us.
You're rid of these
Friggin' birds or rocks or these weeds.
Fall nothing.
It's internal.
Slipping forgetfulness beyond your best intentions.
Well I guess
A slack & empty thing falls internal & looks back.
The extent & list of fault
A slack & empty head for
One loser to sleep in.

Dear Gertrude,

The movie last night showed the characters whole
like in a medical way. So when the man & the woman
were intimate, you saw their whole lives, not just
the moment of power between them. I could stand it
that way.

LONGING FOR PILSNER

So if I'm smart they erase me
Too round to finagle driving
Around your back, turned
More than borrowed for now.
So if I'm smart they erase me.
If time disclosed
Why
Enter the long summer boats
See me bleached down.

BUNGLED FOR AIR

A sound & a touch
A crude new crutch cast for such people.
Head for the famed steams
& it sways brass
Until some hard reasons hedge up & bicker.
Enchanted & round from tumbling thumbs up & pretending
Such a clang of hurt knells
Would be
Be though not remain instead for any animal sighing
For a name, Monday bulletin, same remarkable
Stuff.

let us not to the marriage of true minds admit—

it hesitates—

Dear Gertrude,

So her longing is never filled. So she's sinful. A secret undignified faith she hides from. Not handed down. A thing she creates constantly. So a living thing, not frozen.

So faith as a thing you constantly create. When it's not handed down, you've no home to go back to.

making a sadness & calling it home

In times of weakness, wanting a man's arms to walk into & call that home. As if without it you're false ground, false footing, false courage. But you're not supposed to want it. And the men won't respect you if you want them to love you. So you hide it but you want it, you want it Gert, you do.

IN GOOD HIDING: FOR BLACKIE OF ARCHES DOOR

I know an edgeless old fool
Hunting from a train
Feels bad inside of a red hoard
& better matches stank & stark
"Why me," they ask,
"Spare
This rattling on."
"Ho," we hello
"Rattling on in a new naked city
Would come painless on us.
You could bear it. I am spinning
Round the bend in a whirl."
We have
Such a clean & purposed project, gleaming
On the land.

Dear Gertrude,

More happening today on my own & "completely"
isolated, long hours at the terminal slogging
through songs—& Gertrude, the songs, the songs of
this life are so misleading.

In my dreams a lunatic chased me, I hit him with my
Immaculate candle & he stopped, that dream was
over.

Female saints with their eyes out
Pale saints with the lights out

I prayed a prayer to Our Lady of Under the Roses:

Shelter me under your cloak
the rose of my heart, the rose of my body
Last night the rose at the rise & fall of breath, the last fence before sleep
no gate so you leap it

That song.

So Gert I was up all night again. What sense did it make.

Was my sin loving him more than God? Or love is the *way* to God.

Falling—to leap in faith—this need to be flung—

Noble issue of widespread happiness.

I sleep with this.

singing a long gloved song
long after everyone's gone

SUMMER

A word if imitated
Does impound some or call
Rude night curses on sight & the old profuse drillmen
& a lame lion descending
& other disgraces.
Uncanny lot of fluff
For old reasons lie. Where is the note alarm of reason
Swaying while we sing
The note alarm of reason.

DESCARTES' LAYERS

So soon the tide of loose things
Will scold in the land. Descartes' layers
Will bear this, high or frantic
Proving the land's only a lake of
Figured discards. To speak of this before
Remember what you feel remember
Descartes feels base, bored, such liberty
Shows he cares for the lost one.
So soon the tide of loose things.
                              Old Descartes

Lifts, above this
Unmoving.

So Gertrude,

It gets so lonely I feel like an exaggerated
version of myself. And dream all the time of
leaving my body—it frightens me. *As valuable as a
rope tied to nothing.* But I can't be held
accountable—his music led me to this.

bereft & swimming past the bend of myself

I remember I asked him what do people do around
there. He said *The lake, the long flat land with
its small gray grass in clumps.* It's just nature,
I thought, thinking that town so small it didn't
have much culture. I said what do people do for
entertainment there. T*he taverns. Drink & have
affairs.* Is it nature or culture I wondered.

Things contain their own histories. There is no
land without history & meaning. The ground is
already a narrative—an artifact of intellect—
before people represent it.

this tramped ground
what story the land tells us

SPOKE SONG

The end
      of everything above
The end of everything
         above
Above
      (by all the tall fanning wheels lent from the mill to view the
      thunder cuts through the shape of a ghost & a tired rider)
The end of everything
End of everything
      (sells us lies of wild fame come up from birth
      & wisely buys a big wand a high branch one)
Above. Above. Above. The
End
   of everything
      (can it bear this bluffing raft & mindless luck
      that old bodies long to be late for)

ARMED WITH BEADS FOR TROUBLE

Matter gets us dirty but stands
For alms & bleeds confounded plastic
Of substance. Blue toys
With banners, dashing hooves, we fall or splay
On a wet ridge.
Born in the light of something bent—
But not taken from us—like a day
Does helpless commotion.
Sea call, some sport
Or play of the ridge, we hope
Like a helpless bluebell
On the ridge.

Gertrude, when you say it's the head to be listened
to, not the heart, I can't hear you, what, say it
louder Gertude I can't hear you over the story:

She plays him like a jukebox, any song she wants.
Waving her body. I wanted to drink & be hypnotized.
He kissed her instead of me & I cried
& he said but he's not in love with her it's me
& he kissed her again so it was beginning to be over
& as it was just over one kissed me instead of someone else
& I said don't tell her she'd cry & it would hurt her so
but kiss me again kiss me again I need it kiss me hurry.

She swooned. He exercised a power over her.
She wanted to drink & be hypnotized.

Gertrude. The church says not to fall but sometimes
how can you help it.

I prayed a prayer to Our Lady of Perpetual Help.

Love,
Lisa

headed for relief

YOU'RE BEGGED FOR A PRAYER & YOU FAKE IT

A pounding bird passes all away from us now
Blustering
But just a portent
& yet that prayer
       this paper
         the same
Presume to tenet us
         like a parent
Provokes as a kind of magic.
Birds make us tame
        our selves
Make the paper crumble
        (hi)
If a litany says "God" it's just paper
Makes the prayer sting
A little sore about the creatures that will never be spitting it out
& she
While of a tame magic
Is compost as easily sifted as composure
She
Can't bury the name or her vows
Taking blame
For the diddling of the tame magic.

God favored her with the most wonderful graces,
& she lived in that mysterious sphere to which many saints have been
raised, called the Extraordinary Way.

ONE PIRACY

A violent wind was calling me

Since so many pitied scars lay glistening
To a loud black music. Hissing
Black lawless music.
Each of ten-thousand people lying there.

It calls me while someone else waits for me.
No, why put it so, nor lie
& heave such black loud music. Play
For his mother's pity
Whose mouth would never cry.

It calls me while someone else waits for me.

Or was I willing, a spray flowing dusk, a rind of hope,
Enough I burn silly or bluff my way
Muted, removable, wavering,
Moving.

Gertrude,

I can't write without writing to him but now he can't hear me so who am I writing to.

People say forget, move on, the best is yet ahead & as to this thing between the two of you, the vessel's overturned, possible illness depression & loss.

one door closes, another one opens

We keep trying to use the thing we no longer have. But I didn't choose it Gert, it chose me. Gertrude.

This will be our secret: a fire out back by the shrine & it jumps the ring of rocks, the whole place burns raging out of control.

the men, the men they're so handsome & stern
& sweeping the women up into houses
to hold them & make them woozy

the women, the women cast off by the men,
the men having told them they were only partly good enough

the men, the men telling the women
they were lovely & loved but
the lives of the men needed more & more
devouring the landscape the land
aching countryside rutted
by truck tracks & boot tracks

THE BOOK OF LOSERS

Stunning but our friends, above us
Stars are costly like blue swimmers. Care
To expand? Care has no feeling. No dove has
Liked the notion—which?—its busy old question or its staves' quandaries
For such blue men submerged & costly, or lungs that lie
Like blessed.
Stunning but a friend. Father, I should die, makes amends
A royal coat
Hitched up top unlike him his final pitch amend
Its ending.
Tut, jeweled sea, he could
& some hearts of us could
& the best of us swell, restrained
To bursting. At best,
Hoping blinds without hope.

She was inflamed with love for you, yet she prayed to suffer more,
so great was her love.

Dear Dr. Stein,

I was listening to the voice of a man but he was so
emotional it embarrassed me. Was something wrong
with him. That man was so out of control of his
feelings he hurt me as if I had meant to be hurt.
Did I choose it.

Jack as Jack being Jack

So then he said I wasn't letting go fast enough,
that I have to settle for something in between all
& nothing. That I have to forgive or I am nothing.
It wasn't rational Gert, but Gert I meant well.

Did I read too much into the tenderness when he
spoke?

I wanted to exercise a power over him.

someday someone he will dearly
someone he will love (dearly)
will
some will leave him to go
with another someday
he won't know
what to do someone he will dearly
someday he won't know
how to act someday dearly
he will
someone will dearly

NEW HOMES OF AMAZEMENT

1

Three cheers for the last horizon after our trouble. We escape
        the hell of it & then escape perdition. Quote Paul again. Truer
        was no deed.
One blast resounding as clearly clapped.
Residence hence betrays us, at last
We've got our mouths. So tune a bell for it. We'd like to try
        again. A rock & then a gun.
Best of this course is
Heave-ho &
Tense words.
So soon it's dull (as we live & sleep & keep)
This mood
Has probable
Intentions.

2

Sleeping rooks lie & with each one
We're in a last stand of doltery or a last stand above or a last stand
        to hex. And some we see
Are such there is no vice present.
To be then thirst as acted when bored such lying & say
        we're just as big & as lethal. Weird ugly talk from
        such lying as though two had been one.
Vow to move from this free day to one locked-in kind of
        ward. Or from
This luck we're rolling & we're fast like a devil. Insistence
Being what it is blowing & what you are handed
        & not being measured.
The old last stance, fitful & footloose &
Slow.

the women, the women sobbing
at shrines, at cubicles,
cast about for small purple emblems,
the little amulet nuggets of pain
to press to the skin,
violet glass to press in hard & mean
this is the pain, feel it,
this is the pain, feel it

it's real

My dear one,

He said he's an expert on relationships, he's been
in so many of them, so I fell right in love &
Gertrude you would think I'm crazy but I wanted to
fall, it's true. I had to.

I wanted to promise. To breathe, sing, to believe
in the color of walls, the placement of a flower,
the lyric harmonizing clouds rain window highway
mood and destination. Are women hysterical.

Who has the best manners, who fights fair, is
fairness too impartial dispassionate, doesn't love
require passion hysterical careening proof. It
isn't easy. To have nice days or be wrong for each
other. Enduring & never satisfied. Say please &
want to fix the place up. To rearrange that man &
make him right. To take a rigid conventional
tendency & make it wild. To take a sloppy careless
tendency & make it cautious & kind.

Do you take it as a sign of weakness.

Gertrude, is a saint's body solid, liquid, or gas?

a fire out back & it jumps the rocks,
the whole place burns
raging out of control

**

the saints as martial heroes—
before the martyr became the thing—

See. Gertrude, it all combines.

THIS HOME FOREGOING TREES & PROBLEMS

1

"Blinded trees daring pity
& the final power competes
Cutting through the heart swimming
If it's possible we'll sleep."
At rivers I've been saved from order's curse (as trudging) bereft
      & swimming past the bend of myself. We couldn't casually
Ignore the drop. Trudge along
To arouse them. Removing
This bright truth. This swimming free
Will catch you with fleeting magic. Reach slower then pace. See
The thickened wily old swimmer.

2

Three cheers for the last horizon after our trouble. We escape the
        hell of it & then escape perdition. Quote Paul again. Truer
        was no deed.
One blast resounding as clearly clapped.
Residence hence betrays us, at last
We've got our mouths. So tune a bell for it. We'd like
        to try again. A rock & then a gun.
Best of this course is
Heave-ho &
Tense words.
So soon it's dull (as we live & sleep & keep)
This mood
Has probable
Intentions.

3

My dear, it's your problem these lumber-sluffing doors.
You're coddled so now sluffing low such a wonder such as these it
        does like to stir consternation when at last once you were
        caught & tabled & smart.
            Sea
Heats in the wind. So
Then to resent it.
No
High hopes represent this. The lumber
Refused high hopes. Said
Such bedazzled pullets the high hopes wore. Such
Lies to ourselves. Yet
We insisted.

4

A mind (also called a sin) until rhythm insists on its
        last stand.
We float to ground & belt down an old soul like polite courage
        which, as if one can't tell, is as cute easily as a button.
This can't be such it stands apart within a sort of exact touch &
        heals our limits. Courage lasts to the gate. It's such a
        hunch & tame as a lion. Curls from one lowly old
        boot. The best courage is reason.
In the state of the limit, the rest of it follows double. This
        oldness, this time. Such is what the dove, subtly, flaps.

5

And so let's rest. We catch it & so let's rest without stealing
        a view. Let these tokens
Scheme & hard prefigured, walk
The line. In a labyrinth there's a bone you will play, pick &
special
        offer up your thumb.
Take this advice if you're touring the sagebrush where some
        were livid in spite of lore.
So there's a dark guest who'd leave & walk & still could dine.
        Some king off there touring to go down to
& some that's scrappy or in pottery some bleed to potters wheel
        deathwishes (walks or stalks) so some perplex
        & have to save them
Blind.

6

And so to bed. Where the roddies are angled to get caught
        & dangling on steep lines. Would you bet
About the kings & lancers? Selfless
Goes awry & we shim like twin fins.
For out of sorts depends on the core, care (this spasm),
        caught in its care, or could be caring. So fluttered it
        dangled. A bad deal
& so to bed. The fins
Call us in
Dear.
And all the coasts off the shelf meet the coasts & the shelf glancing
        without moving.
With
Out
Sin.
It could be. And
So to bed.

Dear Gertrude,

In the art of earth against paper, making art of
the earth. In the art of paper pressed to the
stones of streambeds, colored paper the shape of
the stream. Some people love the earth. In the
lament of damage to earth & her streams, the
separation of nature & culture. In the loud song of
our wounding of the earth. But the quiet desert
people of a small continent see no separation. Not
adversarial. Nature is culture. We are married to
earth, though we abuse her. We're married to earth.
Marred.

AT HOME IN A DISH

1

Where I can lie keeping still & smile at all their
        trials.
And awake in the leaves of raw nature.
"It's only me" said I-shall-live to It-is-me. Who immediately hid
        & set me free. I'm free floating for a day of hiding.
Needn't fear for what has been fearful. Needn't touch if it's
        something you've touched in a grey insistence. A slow
        time & so late you can't signal look.
It-is-me can't hide. Because
He objected it was close. (I had a scare because It's-only-me said
        who is It-is-me.) So instead of them I just lie.

2

If I want a fire not a sliver a moment. We like a fire
	blue around
Us about free things.
If not a curse in banding up to lie recklessly
	to old crowds that you were intending for wrestling
To the ground in your plan.
To hurt & to part with also slow leaks (if you fault
	such things) free things in the act of sin. Reveals them
	more like a heroine
Leading the lost way for the blind who are slow.
Furlough on the land of her passion & the land of
	distraction.
A plot for this heroine.

3

When you're pleading for water it makes you think.
        It's them or us, sad
Torture & farther homecomings. By now
None of this likeness insists while you posited
The source, dead or not dead the water would still care. Including
Where something hurts.
Which if you look inside you find the worst enviable.
Including the worst dreams war & its bare sick water slowing to
        refuse us. Altered
Lies & lies of which, source & high dirt,
What will it take? For some
Touch is too late as it should be.
& ladles back the light sources & it takes us. When you're
Pleading for water.

Dear Gertrude,

Our Lady of Just Barely Getting By has visited
again. I can't seem to get rid of her, keep wanting
to tell everyone *look, look* I'm not the same,
something has happened. It's no way to live. My love
becomes a mountain I carry everywhere—pitiful—
grand—magnificent—it weakens me.

I need to be hypnotized. I need to drink to kill pain.

Not wanting hysteria or sainthood ascribed to other
females—

> *the womb wanders restless*
> *throughout the body,*
> *muddled in all its functions—*
> *encouraged by too much*
> *or too little congress with the male*

Gertrude, you weren't there, it didn't make any
sense, the man beating the woman with a 2-by-4, the
woman not leaving the church calling *Brother.* I gave
her kleenex after the candles, the blue Mary's
Immaculate Heart beating exposed & red on her bosom.

Gertrude, *think* about it. What sense did it make,
were we supposed to be there, did we save her.

men suffering their global traumas,
women their inferior constitutions

In the art of the art of the earth, what was he
thinking. Was he thinking.

That man's work bothered me, resting so much in the
beating & hurting of women, the wretchedness of the
male characters. As if his telling it passed for
love or honor. Afterwards, one woman spoke of
another's idea: it's not so much our separation
from each other that hurts us, as our *lack* of it.

that women are too sensitive—
that women are witches—
that sexual pleasure is the root of all hysteria—
that women are blind to each other—

Gertrude: Women's lives. Women's lives. Women's
bodies.

marred

SORE HOPE OF MY HEART

1

Got a bird shouting *Go south* & now if you're smart. If
              there ain't
A cost your belief could win. "We go
Free up & save them," we hate war & closed stores & we're
              leaving in a minute's time you'll dare see. It frees them to
              a purpose keeping true the past judgement & then relief.
"A bad omen just can rot the bad omen's blood."
This is the second you'd dare see invaded by a just hilly land
              when heroes leave. Either
A high urge passes bad omens or doesn't.
Temper looms, harm done looms, hyperbole looms to last
              out the weather below a raging sky.
The sky so thin keeping thin. Can you have the sky's big room
              with an action's small lies & then a vision. Above
Your loss the land transported resistent.
Such are the words you'd dare see. Daunted
By a curse brighter than mild fiction. Because
Sin will bring an infinite peace.

2

A rope I was crying for this one. For some cheater
Bells ring till they cease. "John is so lost he won't know the land,"
　　　　this hill this rock-hold these limes & bay will tease him.
　　　　"Oh stop
Until this lie we'll build a church."
As if I care. Done guessing the mystery at least is done guessing
　　　　luminous. Trudging those, all doubts cast down, cuts the
　　　　moat imported poise too free in the world.
Since you're not alive you leave us. Loss is bound to be for fools.
　　　　Sings red leaves over & under us like blessings.
At least it's lies & some black luminous holes in our land.
　　　　Like it's better.
Can't this, you dolt, prove the reach, can't it promise to break you
Can't it the summit call.

3

If you said darn if you thought of this (can't join with a pretense
     of starting) why are there the shoulders weaving.
     Slow down
Stressed like an afterthought in the worst of some doubts
     that you touch us for whatever muddle.
"Passion on terrace," the louts can't miss if they're singing
     "The Lies Will Bless Us As I Find You." We can invariably
     shop instead buying sounds & solvents.
Where cars go many of us count our blessings for it never bungles
     (you're frowning) & it's so hard we would spill it. Liars
     lie & worse devise for the cases on hand to fall from the
     blessing. It works when the car works. Slow down
Instead either lend the lost one or call it off.

4

Why can't it be removed,
A lost consequence, unstable & blue
About the face or nature of it.
The center of being. Light autumn, about place, no other
        center. About its nature
Out there in the world.
A center of being—caught insisting on old plots.
If he brought it to you, he could make it seem a crisis, & turn it
        into a lesser person sticking through.
White & blond-haired & tan it insists to me even so blundered.
Lost but coming through then, it came with such a war all of us,
        mystery, to call another west insisting love would conquer
        all & as suddenly (too suddenly?) would give up the whole.
When I'm lost on the ice seeking wholeness alone & in love, I
        (with a bleak soreness of mean faces, faces) can't
        resist him.
Cursed Days Home was the title of a handsome book. About
        grace & cause.
Grace!

Her ecstasies became the object of scorn on the part of some,
who to show her as a fake went so far as to pierce her with sharp instruments
& apply lighted candles to her hands.
Yet she prayed to suffer more, so great was her love.
She had frequent ecstasies & visions
until she fell asleep in the Lord.

That *song.*

**

Jack's music & his choosing the birds that sing long notes to the night
after everyone's gone inside. Singing a love that sings a long solo into the
night long after everyone's gone.

Dear Gertrude,

Life is not a completed thing so we struggle to
make sense of it.

the news is bad

Like taking him out of context. And what's on the
inside & what's on the outside for Jack & for his
music & for music & for love & for life.

the sanctuary of perpetual rain
clattering at the windows

Jack got out of his body all right.

MORE BONES & SOME THANK YOUS FOR PORRIDGE & SOUP

1

Failing like a rescue ladder or a goodie tea cup. Hate leaving
       a safe thing?
My eye was dapper, in case you care. So red. "See, with that
       will of hers, I try to be dapper." Too early now
Another unassigned paydirt.
To have to take it or resign around them slugging doors
       or rockabye. Since
I got crazy. Like
So: the pride from beeping big red lines before she seed 'em:
       or there's a tension in most everything: hardly new
       handouts gitchew going screwballs. My request for true
       linament.
Like this, you bend down here & I'll keep humming while
       the fop flies by lost in his mind but heading for the end either
       way. Trouble.
"Learn
This right or you will shovel," one person said,
"Keep yourself hard, see."

2

I could hike or beat my brand around this park.
Lose this flung bitch who puts you through back-hurting
            brawls, or cat calls, hang-ups, or for a fast minute no pain.
            Scum
The bitches who are my age call us. And forget every sorehead
            fears for his life if he has to lose it.
Since lying, what matters beside her, sly faker now steals past
            walls & a new dry dirt to kill this contest. Other guys
            are lying & then they fleece you as you miss dinner, or
            dry out.
So honey it's done. See him go crazy. Why
Botch these homecomings of war & pain, for most of us
We're deceived & since they get to relay us dirty (handy if you
            can stand it) sure
Go & sit locked out of the house,
& take it.

3

Ditches are rotting & seem to accuse you. They behave like ghosts
       of dead people are in them. You sit there without any
       power. While the land to the south hits you with stunners,
       all you have is a black dirtball.
Ignore the signs. They aren't really for you. Fasting outside
       in the dirt. High, actually. And since you're missing, see,
       it's possible. Here what matters is the hike out & you're
       dumbstruck. You better watch it or you won't. You could
       stall for a last wincing haul.
Or bummers in case weather enhances or don't
Around this place
The ghosts of dead people find you highly amusing. The
       ditches in a song accusing, you spook for a hideout
       & leave her nagging you're lying. No, around this place, I
       could swear it's not land.
Commotion
Being interrupted
Jokes
Even when your name is over.

4

God is a big liar & has nothing to do but go at my
        nerves like a big hate line. I'm bloody & caught in hell
        lying here as such this is cruel.
If in these acts the ditch is what matters, then a dapper eye looks
        for a way out. No failed marriage
Is going to eat you out of position like the place exploded &
        no outs, so if you're old or new, it seems a hell
        bound up in this season idling. The reasons
You got bought off playing to them but then you end up caught
        in that huge bright ground on which you are
        drastic.
Yet he's there. As the pain allows you he makes it.
It glows
As if you're the only one who felt its sting.

Dear Gertrude of the Heart, is it wrong to want to be in love all the time. What do you do about it.

Do I read too much into the tenderness when he spoke?

It shifted so the saints looked human. Flesh & blood.

So there's no separation from the earth. That would be leaving the body.

The medical model of love not articulated. Flat. Misproportioned. We know nothing of the lovers, they're just servants of the heart. The most famous doors in the world. Open them & the world is human, bodies & blood, the presence of angels here in our flesh.

Gertrude, would you lose all respect for this woman's passion, would you take it as a sign of weakness.

Chinese boxes inside of boxes.

HEAVEN HOLDS FORTH A LAND MOVER MOST OF ALL

1

Parting with faces all lined up & dry
Was a once-for-all fount of stillness. Stopping to stare &
       lugging blunders. Where leaving the notion can outreach
       the ghost line where the blundering reasons
       want to give you this truth.
You search the line-up for the right reason, a reason, that reason
       felt wrong red & strangely shouted. To hide each
Fact inside the line-up.
Install a building pretty backwards so its waste is intended,
       quite the daring form of distance—viewed from the worst
       waste time, viewed from a time of better waste then,
Who will hear you lean past, the blunders at our backs &
       just as black, in case we have to lie then, in case it is a
       line-up
Just sort of one.
And our pitiful plan as the blunders cough & something small
       counts us under, & it goes on, bleating call of reason,
       once you leave us.

2

A lazier giver wouldn't cover my mistake if she were caught
        in the bin, like all who have come before,
Falling out when she does.
You were bowing out hooking up with a winking front man
Who can blow forth hooked up with a coarse sort of chill just
        like home.
If we can rest initial beats the lost inhabitants would just fall
        Flat, Lost, & Scared-to-See. They changed Flat to
        Lower & Scared-to-See to Pained but left Lost. And
        in summertimes it sits still in a similar fog of
        unanimous figures. Noah
Remained for an ancestor.
You were bowing out hooked up with a winking front man
Who can blow forth hooking up with a coarse sort of chill
        just like home
Or parts, hanging like bells, hardly touch each other in their
        secular journeys.
Suppose for a moment that you could see haze & inflection.
You were bowing out hooked up with a winking front man
Who can blow forth hooking up with a coarse sort of chill
        just like home.

3

Nothing but the best all the way the best holy water on the
       rocks.
It's said the lambs shiver all winter
Nothing but that. The best all the way the best holy water
       on the rocks.

4

Will is a lonely carrier that leaves our shells in a spin.
"If you care put up a fight," they say slowly to no one in the
        least.
Where it spills a laughter the river. Please
Go in there please look & see. So please go in there please
        there. The rest
Is nature. In the lenient
Proof of big & grand & proud
Are all these matters.
Matter of self proud
Til the first ablution
In the best room
No fault the filter caught the lie.

5

They leave us, avoiding harm & odor, but still the angles
       just splay & slide in the spilling gloom.
And so we're parting. To sway
To sway
Off the right bucket.
So high & lazy, we were all lazier when the world wasn't blown
Swaying with it.
Intending not to recover alone.
The host reeling to blow off shining
Alone to recover the sharper
Star, star of any awful martyr
Keeps going, waving.

6

Living & restless spikes of sea-going hawks & without the dread
       we have of late
To care to be here—we can care for hours then scat at a sea-
       going light & leave it.
The sea-going skiff holds to some peg, to hope
Comes intensification. Anyway
We're over that's behind us.
If I were them called out to appear, the skids would remain,
       in the age-old age which is here.
So going alone caring for her, & some peg
Is in its ritual
Now there's the boot & it costs you.
So late.

7

& then it comes all shattered & caught
Wholly caught though it's just a feeling. We've
Erased all the will of us, the stunned what-would-be plucked
          up at last? At best you
Won't shove.
Stay
Without any doubt then & stay once with a skip
& the war & the fights for the sister. And
Swear calling the days' blame. Can't
Find out then that notion. Lonely
& lost to themselves. The leeward
In hock you were sliding for some rounded words. Where this
Will end in a silence. Stiff & lacking
A presence rough in a dark place. We
Miss, with everything, such
Poor plots will still us. Such
Intents are planned, burning.

Gertrude, there's no connection between the ardent
& the desired! No wonder we're always falling!
There's no ground. Like Jack's sad gap between
language & the real.

What's a "chainless" soul? Helium.

Do the women feel, do the men press them to be
close to the feeling. To make a ground to lean on.
Something there.

Jack didn't want a woman to do his feeling for him.
No more gaps, he said. I've had enough.

Then taking him out of context.

The littlest things make the differences later, but
we hurry to our conclusions. The rush to an apparent
ending—but making ourselves less complete.

Black lace of Spanish widows.

ZEN TOMES TO DROWN HEAT

1

"A long sagging trail that looks humbled & trod." Though it's
        un-American to touch with more belief in aspect talking &
        slipping down your hallway toward a slow fall.
"So who'd intend her to get there in spite,
She's lost & lies down there with her other life."
She's spent
Encouraging now & then a slow budding in the minute. No sense
In lying to liars.
Let's toast to something nobody with sense will understand.
        She
Lost then lay down there, fleeing her Other in time—or the
        heat you can't see
Filling the trail way. She cares for most people
Where in sunshine comes floating off behind us. At least
She heard it coming.

2

Bedrock again you face & see to the sea.
Least & best go forth on how it's a cold town seaward. The
        reason it's too cold
& it's small in this without bedrock
Again in the same old bedrock
Again. No holds barred, no cut-run-or-die, no game other than
This.

3

"In due smoke a toxin undone in the fog, in some sanguine
        roofer ran some soft ole song." Like garbage. Like
Country music.
Could we dare ease into tones in dust like that. Like garbage
        & so a quizzing incident will make some dust.
The self. Yet pointless to fight the contest or the needle. "So
        who'd intend her to get there in spite?"
Hope.

4

Til then it's too cold as for where any
Of the cows come mooing & lay near.
Swelling with bum flies oh gnats they convene to get bold.
     Flavor & sin
In a sense. "In the right way such roads from lynch mob to
     candle, decision for a fee was made." And if you face
     collusion force. For these you perk up & lose it or you bolt.
If it's calumny I'll
Spill out in summer since the old bet for its stereotyping or
     they don't get it. I doze injecting those. Now & then
Born again.

5

For Once

I had planned to leave them since the ring won the preposterous
          looseness where we are dangling banter. So
Some of this is missing better you know it. Their ears sealed
          by their new collars.
Once
To write all at once. To dance. I knew I'd be
In the odd word if you hand friends this go telling nothing. Exactly
          concocted in whose pockets.
In this situation, all this riling
& roiled.

6

A tome within the near arch of Hell.
      Any event you see goes against moral choice.
We dance & bring logs like no one else? As if we are no
      one else & discover who loves them. Forego it as an
      area largely written about me as another.
Please invert them. It's our own view of the larger sky so
      bright you can't sing.

7

I'm slowing down near a bump over tears that flow. In search,
       I mean, takes its time while my whiteness looks over
       there. Outspoken & aching with a lot planned so slow it
       spills out. As if
We could take a nation, proud, above all, & without witness.
Earth has caught this notion. If it fails you would miss it
While starting in conquest at better hurts.
It takes the joy of suffering dull-eyed it has begun to climb,
       slowly
In search of more sun. Or hangs on. Oh can't you see such
       dust. Can't
You stand getting the noose tied
Like a man should
Slowly, for my sake, hurt.

8

"Thought I'd just head for the hills," for still hauling logs at
        the chopper & then asking later.
I blamed life.
Watch out for banners, actually, lumped in for my sake. Mistake,
        missed a shot. Bad acts still to call (as if you would
        ask) & it mispelled & all (as if you could miss). Thought I'd just
        head for the hills. It's the middle
Going out blotto who missed & dared.
Red curtains. *Curtains* as they say
So why run away. The runner
Turns a castle & there he's gone & he'll miss breathing. But you
        don't intend for us to tell more since intent is abject &
        startled.
If he calls please hear the just rumbling edgey guilt grief.
        Where along there going down to sin (missing) as
        edgey guilt carpets where you took us. Mis-
Sing fingers, tea & dirt-spill stalled him.

9

Wave (to be in such circuitry) as he hums & calls in a
        fretwork of life.
See (you know it) the lost old victim in a fretwork of life
        while choosing this.
To be free a star it stands red & hot & so long that you
        make a choice. So polite so fleetingly candid so sordid
        & static.
To install in this or make still less of (cagey dare hurls a life
        on) its unimportance.
So its importance is such a joke still the other wish
As above the land reaches another land.
But best of all this
Power, grudge & fury.

10

To bleat oath low to splitting & curses. So scary & weird
        that in fact you despise it. And scary in wild style. It
        won't be through to prove it. A sundered plenty
        universe-full proves it lurching with you. Forward
By necessity since it's not blood that won't be tame
Since who can say. The spider has taken her chances. If you speak
Simple but obdurate. If David lacked
The kind of blood (a hex of blood) that paved a sundered
        plenty proof of lies would send them back. And bled
        the priest then. Lies
Doubt the coughing cold departs & departs & any of this
        departs. Keep yourself hard, see.

Dear Gertrude,

So where is Jack now & his soul, & what is the
bridge & how long the memory & lastingness of Jack,
& how long the contact between two people touches.

And was he in language or in life, or did a long
slow philosophical train cart him around in loops.

This lesson to be gracious & not learning this
graciousness.

The way an older person's music becomes set—it
doesn't stir you up all crazy like the young ones
do. It slips you just a little sideways, an easy
chair with the light shining on *easy* despite the
drummer's grinning return to the unexpected clank.

I haven't lived long enough. What music would Jack
like now—he didn't live long enough—that
agreeable smile part of getting to live so long—

(to be in such circuitry)
as he hums & calls in a fretwork of life

But when the young ones try to play the old ones'
music, it comes out muddy.

Or Jack as Jack always wanting it different &
heading for his own bitter implosion.

Dear Jack,

This lesson to be gracious & not learning this
graciousness.

No wonder we're always falling.

There's no ground.

ABOUT THE AUTHOR

Lisa Cooper has lived most of her life in Tucson, Arizona, and is a graduate of the MFA program in Creative Writing at the University of Arizona. Chax Press has published two chapbooks by Cooper, *The Ballad in Memory* and *Tilt Rail*. Cooper works as an editor with Madden Publishing. She can frequently be found at musical events in Tucson and is a member of the organizing committee for Zeitgeist, a presenter of innovative jazz concerts.

& Calling It Home is Lisa Cooper's first full-length book.

Other Chax Press Books

Phillip Foss, *Chromatic Defacement*
Diane Glancy, *A Primer of the Obsolete*
Lydia Davis, *Blind Date*
Lisa Cooper, *Tilt Rail*
Rae Armentrout, *writing the plot about sets*
Tenney Nathanson, *One Block Over*
Tom Raworth, *Three Poems*
  & Charles Alexander, *Pushing Water* (in one volume)
Bob Perelman, *The Masque of Rhyme*
Hank Lazer, *3 of 10*
Tom Mandel, *Prospect of Release*
Myung Mi Kim, *The Bounty*
Mary Margaret Sloan, *The Said Lands, Islands, and Premises*
Kathleen Fraser, *when new time folds up*
Norman Fischer, *Precisely the Point Being Made*
Nathaniel Tarn, *Caja del Rio*
Rosmarie Waldrop, *Fan Poem for Deshika*
Lisa Cooper, *The Ballad in Memory*
Nathaniel Mackey, *Outlantish*
Ron Silliman, *Demo to Ink*
Beverly Dahlen, *A Reading 8-10*
Gil Ott, *Wheel*
Karen Mac Cormack, *Quirks & Quillets*
Susan Bee & Charles Bernstein, *Fool's Gold*

Sheila Murphy, *Teth*
bp Nichol, *Art Facts: A Book of Contexts*
Charles Bernstein, *Four Poems*
Larry Evers & Felipe S. Molina, *Wo'i Bwikam/Coyote Songs*
Mei-mei Berssenbrugge, *Mizu*
Charles Alexander, *Hopeful Buildings*
Lyn Hejinian & Kit Robinson, *Individuals*
Eli Goldblatt, *Sessions*
John Randolph Hall, *Zootaxy*
Paul Metcalf, *Firebird*
Karl Young, *Five Kwaidan in Sleeve Pages*
Charles Alexander, *Two Songs*
Paul Metcalf, *Golden Delicious*
Jackson Mac Low, *French Sonnets*